How to Make More Money

11 Ideas to Build Extra Income

Plus

10 Ways to Make Money Online

Entrepreneur Series

Saad Ghafoor and John Davidson

Mendon Cottage Books

JD-Biz Publishing

All Rights Reserved

Disclaimer

Warning

Check out some of the other Entrepreneur Series books
Entrepreneur Series books on Amazon
Check out some of the Science of Living Series books
Science of Living Series on Amazon
Check out some of the Health Learning Series books
Health Learning Series on Amazon

Table of Contents

Introduction 4
Chapter 1: What is Your Attitude about Money? 6
Chapter 2: Passive and Active Income: What's the difference? 9
Chapter 3: Things to Consider In Building Extra Income 11
Chapter 4: 11 Ideas to Build Extra Income 14
    Sell some stuff online 14
    Be an agent for selling cars, houses and lots, apartments, condos, and
    other things. 14
    Turn your hobby into cash. 15
    Make a Blog or Develop a Website 15
    Have some part time work or job. 16
    Own some vending machines 16
    Breed some pets, dogs, cats, or whatever animal 16
    Invest some of your monthly income into the stock market 17
    Make your own invention or products 17
    Open a car washing service in your garage. 17
    Engage in Beekeeping 18
Chapter 5: Building Extra Money Booster 20
Chapter 6 - Bonus - 10 Ways to Make Money Online 22
    Way 1: Think About Selling Products Either Yours or Others 22
    Way 2: Selling Digital Products with Clickbank 28
    Way 3: Developing an Etsy Shop to Sell Amazing Crafts 31
    Way 4: Developing Career on oDesk – Selling Your Skills 32
    Way 5: Are you A Creative Writer? Join iwriter.com or iNeedArticles .. 34
    Way 6: Fiverr.com Can Help a Lot 36
    Way 7: Writing Kindle Books to Sell on Amazon 38
    Way 8: Have a Teaching Passion? Teach Others Online 40
    Way 9: How You Can Flip Websites on Flippa 41
    Way 10: How to Double Your Money Using Online Resources 43
Chapter 7 - Reasons for Online Business Failure 45
Conclusion 46
Author Bio 48

Introduction

In today's economy, it is a wise decision to learn how to build some extra income. Sticking to your paycheck alone from your day job isn't secure anymore. Some people experienced sudden layoffs from their employers and they ended up desperate and shocked. Aside from that, upon building extra income, you can add more money into your savings and investment accounts that will truly work for you in the future.

Therefore congratulations for taking some time reading this eBook about how to build extra income. This is your very important first step to learn how to live with different streams of income. You have probably heard about **financial freedom**. Many people often love this. They want to be free from the bondage of money problems. Yes, money is not enough for a lot of people. Yet, you are different from them because you believe that there's a way out for this problem.

So, in this book you will learn a lot of ways and tricks on how to build more income. To be specific, this book will

- ✓ Condition your mind to have the right mind setting to acquire more money

- ✓ Explain to you the difference between passive and active income

- ✓ Give you 11 money making ideas to build extra income with a clear discussion

- ✓ Give you some tips on how to handle extra income without sacrificing your health

- ✓ Help you unleash your very own creativity to build more income

This book provides simple yet comprehensive guidelines in building extra income. It will also boost your inner confidence about money itself. In short, you will learn how to carefully choose a wise decision in order to build extra income. It will also teach you not to waste your time on unsuccessful ways of earning some extra income.

This book will mold your whole personality when it comes to building extra income. And, it will also prepare you to embrace the important points to consider when choosing the right ways to earn.

This book will let you remember your forgotten talents, capabilities, creativities, knowledge, skills, and everything about you that can make a difference in making more income. Who knows, you can turn that extra income into a super income that could replace your day job. Well, that is not impossible!

But for now, let's stick to first building extra income. This book will really help you pay your bills fast, save you more money, or can give you more money for a brand new vacation, and a lot more.

By the way, what is the reason why you want more income? What I want you to do is write it down in your personal book to make it a guide or goal. You can post it in your room or put it on the refrigerator. Just be honest to yourself. This will only serve as your motivation or inspiration for you to strive more in building extra income successfully.

Chapter 1: What is Your Attitude about Money?

I will ask you a question, what is money to you? What is the real value or score of money in your life? Does it have a great impact to you and your family?

Well, I know your answer is probably, "YES". But, the reason I ask it to you is for you to check it into yourself, once again, why you are interested in learning to build extra income.

Yes, your reasons could be from these options:

1. You run out of money because your paycheck isn't enough for paying a lot of your bills and debts

2. Your money is just enough for all your needs and you need some extra money to buy some of your luxuries

3. Your money is just enough for all your needs but you want to have some savings

4. Your money is enough for your needs, wants, and savings, yet you love spending too much because you are shopaholic

5. You have enough money for everything; but you want some more money to make you very rich

You can have your own choice different from the above list, and let's evaluate each option.

For option number one, well, congratulations! That means you are a problem solver and that's a good sign of progress. Sometimes you don't need to blame yourself, because today's economy is really bad. That's why your paycheck isn't enough money anymore. But, do know you that there's a good thing about this situation? You become aware that you can do something for yourself without relying too much on your paycheck. And you can prove to yourself that you have something within you that you can use to protect yourself from this bad economy.

Option number two is different. Your motive is for your wants and passion. Well, people have different priorities. Many want to enjoy life to the fullest without minding their savings first. They are just contented of meeting needs and wants. But I tell you, this is dangerous. You should have some savings as your emergency fund for unexpected events where you may need some extra money.

To continue, let's have a look at option number three. Well, you are a good man or woman. You think about savings and that's a good sign of valuing and giving respect to money. That means, you are a good steward according to what the Bible says. So, it's a good shot.

And for option number four, I will say it's too bad for you. Your money is enough for your needs, wants, and savings yet your money will not be in its proper places because you spend it all. Thus, you end up ruining your budget and ruining your life. I tell you, money really matters in this world. Yes, money is not everything, but without it you cannot get nor have something. Practically speaking, you need money as your purchasing power to buy all your needs. We are not living in the prehistoric era where survival was different. So, I suggest, it is better to change your attitude about money first. Please forget the addiction of having to buy that next shiny object or the pleasure you feel while buying or shopping. Learn to control your impulse shopping. That pleasure is only a super trick that most businesses have preprogrammed and marketed to get your hard earned money. Therefore, make sure to buy things which are important and necessary for you to continue your normal life. By doing this, you will be proud of yourself even more. Learn to control money don't allow it to control you.

Last but not the least is option five, you got it! You are financially wise and have learned to control your money. I hope your motive to be rich is not only for yourself; but also for others.

So, all these options only show your attitude towards money. The more you use and keep your money well; the more financially mature you are. I hope you will not end up keeping or saving your money only, but also investing it for better results.

But, going back to building extra income, now you are sure of yourself and know why you need to earn extra income. Therefore, try to become more motivated. Be willing to do and take the risks because you know your goals and motives. And most of all, it is because you need to help yourself.

Chapter 2: Passive and Active Income: What's the difference?

While you are very excited about building passive income, let's talk first about INCOME. Income means money that comes in your hands from different sources. But, now I will make it clear to you that there are two kinds of income. These are the **passive** and the **active** types. So, what makes the two different from each other?

The meaning of each word speaks for itself. First, **active income** is the money that you can get from an active source of income. That means you work hard for it so that money will show up. On the other hand, **passive income** is the money that comes in even if you don't literally work for it. It just comes in even when you are sleeping or not working at all.

To give you a concrete example about how these two work, I will share something. The paycheck that you receive from your regular job is an active income. But, when you are investing in a company and you have a dividend every year, that money is passive. But mind you, investing in a company is only one among the thousands and thousands of ways of earning passive income. Paintings, antiques, gold, old coins, hotels, apartments, books, stocks, etc. could be good passive income sources.

So what about it? Maybe you are thinking that your only concern is just having extra money. Wait… this is your eye opener to find a better way of finding extra income that will not ruin your time, health, family time, career, and your other priorities in life.

There are a lot of people out there who are too busy, even late at night, just to earn some extra bucks and they end up getting sick or distracted. Following these guys isn't a wise thing to choose if you really dream of something more relevant than extra pennies only.

Working smart is far better than working too hard for money. If you are not wise you will simply become a slave for money in the end. Yes, you will become a slave because you are going to sacrifice everything, even your very own life, family, career, health, and other priories just to get that **"extra"** money.

So, which one is better? You know the answer. Check yourself if you have enough time to do either an active or passive income. Check your health if you can do more active than passive income. Just try checking all the angles in your situation. Do what is best and wise for your situation.

I'm just giving you the idea that there are many ways to make money even if you have a very limited amount of time, shaky health, a big family, serious work, etc. Using or choosing among the two is good enough for you to build the extra income of your very own desire. And if this makes you comfortable enough, compare to others who are already burnt out working for that extra money.

Therefore, from now on, make a careful evaluation about yourself to which kind of income that you want. Understand and analyze all the advantages that you can get in order for you to have a clear picture of yourself in terms of getting extra income. After that, the next step will not be so hard for you to follow.

Chapter 3: Things to Consider In Building Extra Income

Like any other ventures, building extra income has some things to consider. This will make you more prepared, ready, available, knowledgeable, and organized. In doing so, money will follow quickly because it is carefully planned and organized.

So, how are you going to start building your extra income?

1. **Know your skills, knowledge, talents, and other expertise.**

   This is the most important device when you consider earning some extra money. It is just like asking yourself "what do you have to give in exchange for cash?" Isn't it a bright idea? Take note that in every skill, talent, knowledge, and expertise that you have, you can always make money from them. So, the more you have the wider the scope of your money making capabilities.

   For example if you are good at English, you can be a tutor, writer, blogger, etc. If you are good at sketching and drawing, you can offer special services for this in your very own home or write a book. If you know how to repair computers and other electronics, then there are a lot of people who want your service. There are thousands of ways on how to use what you have in order to make extra money.

2. **Know your real worth.**

   How much are you worth right now? Do you have money set in a special bank account? Do you have savings already? Well, if you are a risk taker, you can use some of your savings as a startup capital for a small business as your **extra income maker**. This time, the idea of **passive income** comes in. It is true that **money makes money if you know what you are doing**. There are some small businesses that only need a little of your time, yet the return is big enough. For example, if you have enough money to build an apartment complex, then that's a good source of extra income that comes in monthly. But, if your money is not that big then there are hundreds of ways to start a small business. You can even have a vending machine that sells candy.

3.   **Know your availability and willingness.**

Will you devote extra hours for this extra income challenge? Are you committed enough to follow this schedule every day? Are you not too busy for this extra work? Will your wife, husband, family allow or support you in this thing? Seriously, will you take all the responsibilities just to make things work for this extra venture? So, answer those questions for yourself. Building extra money needs time and availability. You must be consistent and true in it because you need to take care of it. Remember that you are also building your reputation and your portfolio. And once you treat this extra income well, it could become a very good business opportunity for you. Therefore ask yourself if you are really serious about it.

4.   **Check your health status.**

This does not mean that you should be 100% healthy. This only means that you need to choose the right kind of extra income that will truly fit your health condition. So, consult a doctor first if it is advisable to you to work extra or limited hours every day. And ask yourself if the activities that you are going to do will affect your sickness, if any. So, be very careful, as health is the best wealth among all. Life is more precious than money alone. You can never enjoy your money without having a good health.

There are still many other things to consider when it comes to building extra income, but these four things are the most important. So right now, ask yourself these four things. Then be very honest in answering all of them so that there will be no problems in the future. It is always a wise decision to think it over before starting something that can really have a great effect in your life.

Chapter 4: 11 Ideas to Build Extra Income

There are thousands of different ways on how to build some extra income. Below I will share some examples that are very applicable to anybody. And through these ideas, you will also realize that you can make your own creation using your very own creativity. Actually, it takes only some common sense, creativity, knowledge, organization, a great system, and lots and lots of hard work.

So, choose what will be the best fit for you and learn its ways. Remember that any of these ideas could be a passive or active source of income. So, just understand each of these very well.

Sell some stuff online

While living in this Information Age, one needs to take advantage of the use of the internet as a powerful tool in earning some extra income. There are many powerful websites that you can use for this such as Amazon, EBay, and other local websites in your area. You can sell some of your old things or some stuff that you don't need at all. You can also intentionally buy something from thrift stores, garage sales, flea markets, and other shopping stores in order to sell online. EBay is a very good site for everyone to start earning online. It has lots of surprises because whatever you sell, there is always a possibility that it will really sell even it's weird. There are many people who make a living by selling on EBay, but of course it took a lot of hard work and learning for them to succeed. For you, start small and learn how it works. Observe and understand the structure and its entire process. Look at the other sellers and observe what they are doing. Try researching for some improvements and get inspired by people who succeed from doing it and learn from them. In the end, you will reap the benefits of your hard work. So, if you love selling without too much work, go for online selling.

Be an agent for selling cars, houses and lots, apartments, condos, and other things.

This is a very good side project that will give you a lot of extra income. You can do this anywhere, even when you are at work. This will work best if you know a lot of people who have a lot of money. And most of all, this will work if you have the talent and skills in making sales talk. Yes, if you are good at making friends and talking to different kinds of people, then this is a very good idea for you. And mind you, you will get a handsome amount in a very little percentage only. Houses and lots have high prices, so if it will be sold you'll get a lot of money. It will take some training and to sell houses you will need to get a license in most places. In my area it is a 3 month course and then you have to pass a test.

Turn your hobby into cash.

This is a fast cash income generator for you. If you love painting, writing, gardening, cross-stitching, cooking, sewing, dancing, singing, or any other talent, you can also make money out of it. But how can you make it? Well, it's too easy. You can always offer some personal services to your friends, neighbors, church mates, officemates, and to other people that you know and even people you do not know. Your hobbies could be exchanged for money if you offer them as your services. For example, you can cater your friend's birthday party if you are very good in cooking. And, if you are good in writing, you can find some people who need a writer or an editor. You can offer that service especially to college students who are too busy doing a lot of paper work. For cross stitching, you can do this in your spare time and make items beautiful and big enough for you to sell it at a very good price. Your friends and neighbors could be your first clients for this. There are so many ways to earn money from your hobby. Even through your garden, you can get some extra cash. Just try finding different ways to market the product of your hobby. My sister is very good at sewing and loves to make dresses. She has made hundreds of dresses from wedding to formal gowns and she has now built up such a reputation that people are calling her and she has a waiting list of people requesting here services. I love to build with wood and I am getting calls all the time from people wanting me to make cabinets and things for them.

Make a Blog or Develop a Website

If you love the online world of blogs and websites, then you can go for this. However, it takes a lot of work, especially in setting up a website. For blogs, you can start easily and you can monetize slowly. You can have Google Ad sense for its advertisements and you can promote affiliate products for you to earn money. Actually, this is a very good passive income if you know how to make the whole process without doing it alone. You can hire someone and you can capitalize money to take care of it. Some people hire virtual assistants who will do the work for them because they are busy doing their regular job. Some people earn hundreds and thousands of dollars using their blogs and websites. If you are curious about it, you can research online and you can buy some books to gain useful knowledge that will give you the step by step process. It is always an advantage to have a better background for this, with enough time and money in order for you to earn fast. So, invest wisely for this and if the return is big enough, you may even quit your job.

Have some part time work or job.

If you have some hours to do some part time jobs, then it is also good idea. This can even give you more exposure, more connections, and more experience. If you are a teacher, you can teach in other colleges or universities during the evenings. And if you are a secretary, you can have some extra jobs in other companies for a few hours in the evening only. If you want, you can be a part time sales lady, bartender, tour guide, lecturer, assistant, nanny, caretaker, gardener, dog walker, etc. There are many ideas for you to apply for a part time basis only.

Own some vending machines

Vending machines are awesome because they are like money machines. This machine works very well even when you are not there. You can build or put it in a place where people usually hang out or stop by. You can put it in a store, shop, hospital, school, or anywhere people will notice it. Just make sure that you know and trust the owner of the store or the place where you will leave your vending machines. And for the products, you will just choose what you are most comfortable selling. Even candies will work for this. Just imagine owning 3 or 5 vending machines that each gives you a $100 everyday. Wow, then you can have $400 a day without working a lot for them. Then multiply that into 30 days. And that's a pretty $12000.00 amount of passive money. Math will really do the work if you will just allow it to happen.

Breed some pets, dogs, cats, or whatever animal

If you are pet lover, then this is a very good extra income. I set this idea aside because breeding pets could be very lucrative, and only a few people do. So, start buying some good breeds of dogs that you love and take good care of them until they will have babies. Then, make sure that you have enough space with good ventilation. Make sure to send them also to a veterinarian for their regular checkups. If you think they are pretty much ready, you can then sell them. Just choose the dogs that will give you a good sale price. Dogs are one good example; but you can add your own choice of animals, even snakes. Make sure you check into the rules and regulations in your area for any regulations for kennels or raising animals.

Invest some of your monthly income into the stock market

Please don't think twice about it. I will not suggest investing a huge amount of money for this. Just set aside an amount that you are most comfortable investing, and try thinking that it is your savings. Actually, this income is for a long term goal. Let's say for 10 or 20 years down the road. Take note that in your savings account, the interest rates are small compared to the stock market. So, what you will need to do now is to research and start picking the strong, stable, big, and profitable companies, and invest monthly. Just choose three or five trusted companies and they will give you a good rate of return in the future. For sure, this is a very good passive income that can go with your other sources of extra income.

Make your own invention or products

Well, you don't need to be like Thomas Edison for this. Just try thinking about what you can create that other people would be happy to use also. It does not need to be a sort of technology, because anything will do. Just like making your own bracelets, clothes, curtains, cookies, cakes, candies, jam, décor, clip, balloons, souvenirs for weddings, books, and many others. It is just thinking of your skills again, but this is product centered. After this, go and sell your product, that's it.

Open a car washing service in your garage.

This is a little weird, but it doesn't mean that it should always be in your garage. If you have some space, you can always use that for that service. You can set your washing hours in which you are free to offer your service. If you offer a cheaper price compared to the other car wash centers, then you'll have more customers. This mini business is very easy to set up and has a low cost. Just get a permit if you are getting serious about and if you have a lot of returning customers. You could also start a mobile wash business where you travel to them and wash their cars.

Engage in Beekeeping

Bees are weird too, but if you are in a good place where you can set up a beekeeping area, then go for it. Bees mean honey for sale. And most people love the idea of having fresh and authentic honey from a person that they know very well. Aside from that, many people will be interested in your activity. You can even extend your bee farm into a real farm where you can have some chickens and other animals that you like. If you are an animal lover, this is a great idea for you. We have chickens and my wife sells the extra eggs to neighbors.

There are a lot of ways to earn extra income. Just open your eyes, mind, heart, and strength to build it well. Some could be unexpected and weird, yet they are worth doing. So, don't underestimate some of your ideas because everyone has his or her own unique money making thinking, that if put into practice, then it will be a big surprise. You will never know unless you try it. Money is in the mind and it is your willingness if you will take the challenge, as well as, the risk to make a start of it. Now, speaking of **"willingness"** that's a tough word for you to do. Doubts may creep in your room tonight and will delete all these things that you've read. So, to continue, learn how to boost yourself in building extra income in the next chapter.

Chapter 5: Building Extra Money Booster

You are here learning about making sure the things that we are tackling will happen. Are you really convinced that all these things will work? Do you have doubts right now? Well, I'm not pushing you to say yes, because you should be honest to yourself, but I will say that it is a normal thing to **starters and beginners to be a little doubtful**.

So, you are a starter and please accept the truth if you are. A starter needs to learn the ropes of many things. But, do you know what the good thing of being a starter is? A **starter has a fresh mind with a little seed of hope to dream bigger**. According to the Bible, if you have a seed of hope, you can move mountains. That little hope and faith of yours can make you what you are. If you persist, then you'll win. But, if you are afraid to start, you will never fail because you don't actually start. Therefore, never be afraid of failing because failure will give you valuable lessons.

I do not say that I want you to fail, but just don't be afraid of it. Successful people's backgrounds were never a bed of roses. They were not living a perfect life before. But, they turned their scary past into a fruitful future by working hard for it and learning lessons. So, accept the challenge and keep trying and doing the things that you believe, because you have a dream. One step at a time, many people will say. Yes, it could be because there's always a need to begin. So, just do it and do it well.

Building extra income is pretty easy to people who are not closing their doors to different opportunities. So, please don't doubt yourself. Believe that there is something in you that can make your extra income a real income that could even replace your monthly income one day. Just work for it and work for it again. Just don't limit yourself to things that you want to try in making extra money. If you have the feeling, instinct, or the gut to do it, then follow it. I tell you, humans have powerful instinct that if followed, results would be huge. And you are in that position right now.

Upon reading this book, you already followed your instinct to search for a tool in order to materialize your goal in building extra income. So, pat yourself for making your first step worth reading.

Chapter 6 - Bonus - 10 Ways to Make Money Online

Way 1: Think About Selling Products Either Yours or Others

With the internet becoming the most supportive tool in earning money by sitting almost anywhere in the world, opportunities have spread significantly for individuals who acquire diversified skills and can execute them to earn an additional amount for themselves. Time after time one incredible job after another has been created by people who possess an expertise in selling products. Now, if one does not have his/her product to sell what happens then? Does the talent go to waste? No, you can sell others' products just the same way you would have done if it they were your own and earn the compensation for the effort that you have put in to generate the sales or leads of your employer.

How We Could Use Marketing Channels

Running an online business can be a dream come true. Starting a business without or with minimal investment, no human resource requirements, and a very small chance of financial loss, can be very appealing.

First Phase: Organize.

Second Phase: Look for attractive opportunities and programs.

Third Phase: Become part of the selected program.

Fourth Phase: Gain keyword knowledge.

Fifth Phase: Draft an Adword Ad on Google.

Sixth Phase: Launch an Adword campaign.

Seventh Phase: Monitor performance and response to the ad campaign.

Affiliate Marketing

The most prominent marketing of today on the internet is affiliate marketing, which refers to the connection between an online retailer, who has products that he/she wants to sell, and the affiliates, who will assist in selling the products. The affiliate's work is to get the advertisements of the retailer's product to convert into sales. In simpler words, affiliates attract traffic towards the retailer's product. Each sale or lead will have a certain amount of money that is associated with it and the higher the number of successful leads, the higher the earnings.

To sell someone else's product, or become an affiliate, you can start by signing up at an affiliate program, which is offered by multiple online companies. However, there is another way you can opt for, which is by joining as a member of an affiliate network. In some cases, to sell the product of someone, you will have to have a website of your own, which will provide all the information related to the product that you'll be affiliating. This helps in providing an authentication statement to the employer, making them acknowledge that you know what you're up for, and acquire ample knowledge to promote the product and generate leads out of it. Moving onwards, there will be a certain type of affiliate marketing program that you have aimed for, and that will decide the amount of money you'll be able to make per month.

Google Pay Per Click

- It provides a fast response by receiving immediate clicks from search engines. In a day or two, you can get the exact position on your business.

- By paying the right amount, you can receive lots of potential traffic through search engines to your website.

- By using this method, it is easier to keep an account of the exact number of people visiting your website.

Pay Per Click and other CPA Marketing Tactics

There are multiple programs amongst which PPC (pay-per-click) advertising and CPA marketing come under. CPA marketing refers to Cost per Action that comes under affiliate marketing, wherein the affiliate's task is to generate leads for the merchant's product. The affiliate is only paid if the advertisement generates a lead i.e. brings some action into the work. The amount of money that you can earn also depends on how strong the competition is in the market that your product falls. For example, in an insurance policy affiliate program the competition will be high, but at the same time if you're able to generate a lead in such a competitive market, you'll earn a healthy compensation for the intense hard work. To drive traffic towards the retailer's product the affiliate can buy several ads from different marketing websites such as Clickbank and Facebook. You can even create a Facebook page of your own where you'll be promoting the products and developing a good customer relationship. Other ideas might include creating a blog and finding related websites where you can post the retailer's ads.

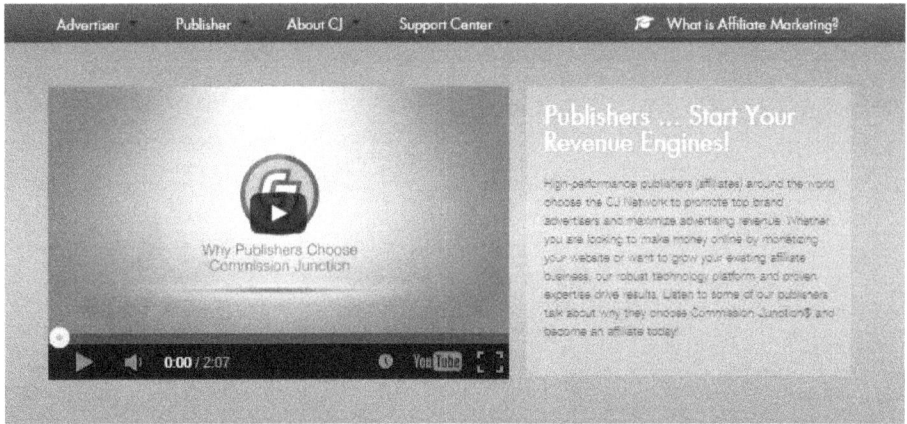

Why Publishers Choose Commission Junction

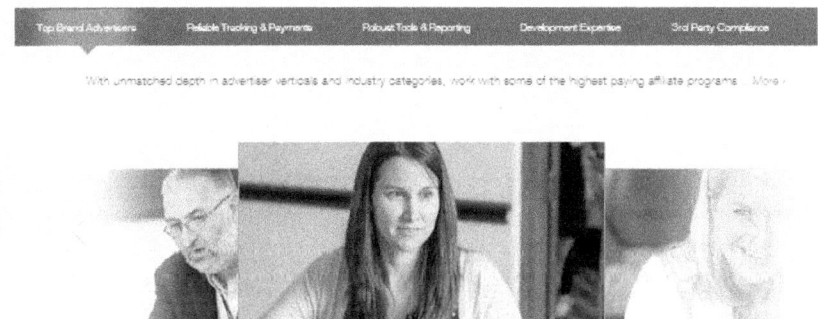

http://www.cj.com/

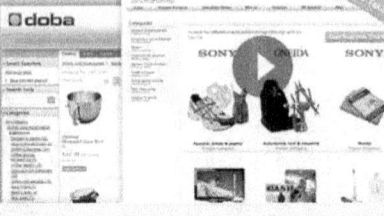

http://www.doba.com/

Marketing Channels and Auction Sites Just as eBay

Success of one medium of communication and marketing in a business may not last for some other forms of business entities. Use of different mediums of selling and marketing one's products increases the profitability and survival chances.

- One of the advantages of using multiple channels of marketing is that it increases your visibility to the customer.

- This book provides suggestions about different channels of marketing and reaching your customer. You have to select the best-suited option for your business. For example, if you are an online start up business, you can use eBay as a channel for selling your product. In addition, as you grow you can move to other channels as well.

Some of the marketing and promotional strategies that online businesses are currently using may include the following:

- Using online auction services to sell your product.

- Use of discount channels like Overstock.com.

- You can sell your products through merchant websites like Amazon.com.

- You can create your own web store.

- Use the services of other web stores.

- Use the strategy of pay per click through search engines to divert traffic to your website.

- Follow the strategy of search engine optimization and avoid paying per click fees.

- Integration of online and offline operations can help boost sales and business profitability through efficiency improvement.

- If you are using affiliate websites, you can pay commission to them and enhance your business through increased customer base and traffic.

- Use of email and instant messages to send newsletters can help increase potential customer base and spread the information about new products and sales promotions.

- Using social networking sites and discussion groups to spread the business message to clients.

Advantages of Using Auction Sites/eBay to Sell Your Products:

The following are a few reasons for using eBay as a selling channel:

- It has a large number of users.

- A large number of success stories have been linked with eBay. Many individuals are earning from this medium and growing over time.

- It is user friendly and allows easy access to product campaign postings. Starting on eBay is very convenient and easy.

- It provides various options for the seller. You can use an auction strategy, or sell at a fixed price. There is also a web store and a main listings category.

- It provides secure transaction methods to its customers and sellers. For example, PayPal buyer protection and eBay Standard Protection.

- Transactions can be made through PayPal accounts and credit cards.

Timing Strategies:

When using an auction mode for selling your product, choosing the right time and duration is vital. Below are some guidelines in this regard:

- EBay experiences more user traffic on weekends and in evenings. Therefore, you should plan and extend an auction during this time period to enhance chances of sales.

- Larger time periods mean more viewer ship and more potential clients. However, popular products require lesser time and more demand.

Way 2: Selling Digital Products with Clickbank

Everyone has their own talent they want to work with and acquire an expertise in, but sometimes they might not get a platform to do so. Writers are an important part of our community and deserve to earn by the remarkable talent of being able to write marvelously on multiple topics. Clickbank provides the ultimate platform for such people who can develop their own digital products and sell them on the Clickbank website. Digital products refer to software, eBooks, articles, magazines, PSD templates, and Word Press themes that one can develop. The topics can be diversified, and you can write on the topics of which you have genuine knowledge.

Clickbank is amongst the best websites to sell your digital products, because it gives plentiful features that one would like to see in effect. They have a large network of affiliates, who will advertise your products to related customers and generate a lead to make the sale of your digital product a reality. It really helps those who know precisely know how to write and who are incredible at it, but do not want to go through the tedious process of advertising it and trying to sell it somewhere. Once you have posted your product on Clickbank, it will be the job of affiliates to make a sale happen and generate the income.

We have done really well with the websites that we have set up and used the Clickbank Marketing structure.

Here are a few of our sites

http://housecabin.com

http://pdfbarns.com

http://plansforplayhouse.com

http://bunkhouseplans.com

Http://hplans.us/blog

http://pdfgarages.com

http://www.build-chicken-coop.com/

http://cabinplansanddesigns.com

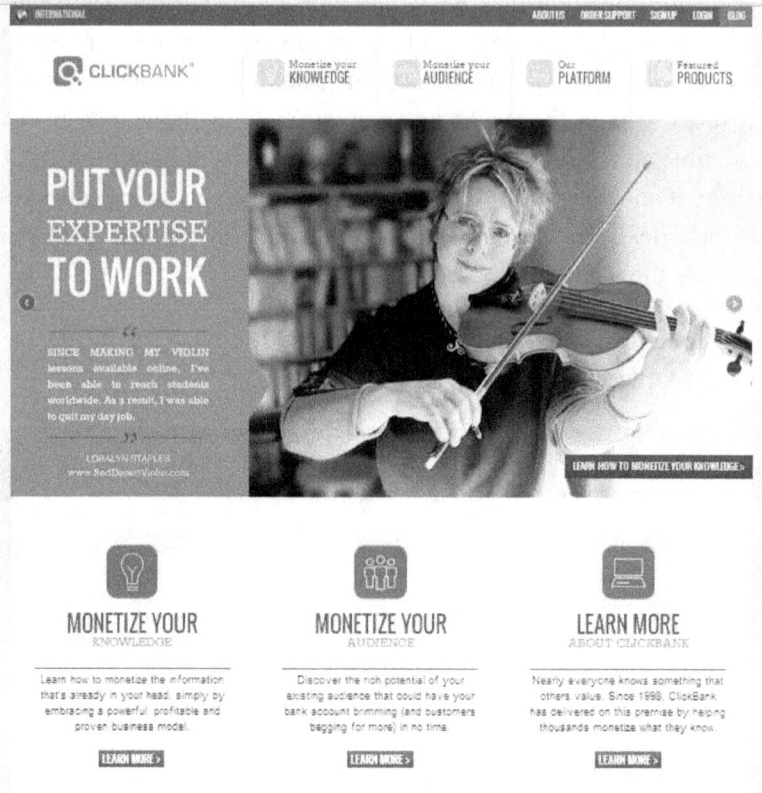

http://clickbank.com

If you're trying to make a healthy amount then you can add as many products as you wish and generate the income. The selling price of each product is up to you and Clickbank doesn't impose any restrictions on it. For each product that is sold, minor compensation is cut for providing the services. To set up an account at Clickbank, you can visit the website and find all of the information on the process. The requirement of your own website has to be fulfilled before you can start selling your products. The website will house all of the information and a description about your product, a link that connects your website to Clickbank and a thank you page. Once you're set with the website, you can keep adding your work and also connect with customers through it.

Way 3: Developing an Etsy Shop to Sell Amazing Crafts

Do you have the creative seed in you? Do you possess the talent to improvise and make something beautiful out of a mere ugly product? Do you have a vintage item that still has incredible appeal within it? Etsy is the place for you to sell all the incredible and beautiful products of your creation and earn money. Etsy is a website, which offers handmade, vintage items made by suppliers of arts and crafts. An individual can sell his/her art, photography, outerwear, designed jewelry, quilts and much more. Any product that you have created by using your incredible creative brain, you can add to your shop at Etsy for sale.

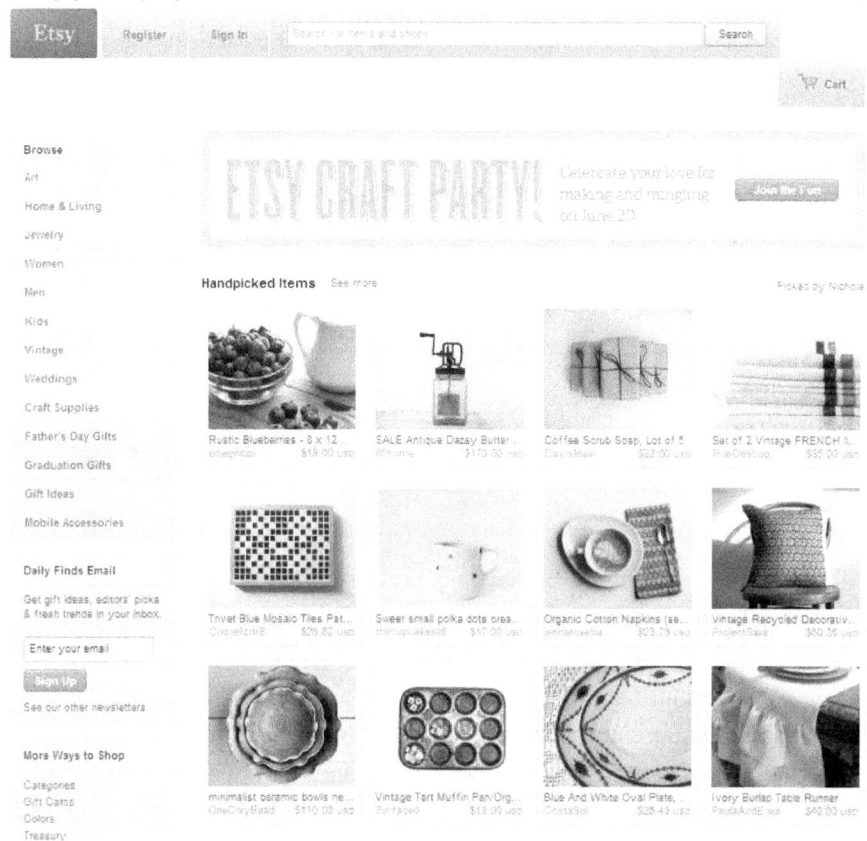

http://www.etsy.com/

The first step is to create your own shop on the Etsy website. A username will be asked for and then a shop name through which you'll be known. You can use any name that you think will define the products on your shop at its best. Be very careful about the username you chose because you'll not be able to change it later. To attract customers you need to offer some uniqueness in your product and you can do that by using your creative skills to come up with something that others are not selling. A recommendation to all the potential Etsy shop owners is to always take good pictures of your product, because the visual image of your product at first sight is what appeals to customers and motivates them to want to buy the product.

The biggest advantage of using Etsy is that they do not charge you for opening a shop at their website. For entry to an amazing world of creativity, Etsy has made selling an act that is free of cost. However, for every item that you add into your shop, $0.20 is incurred for a period of 4 months. If you're willing to keep it for a further few months, the costs will be incurred at the same rate. For each successful sale made, Etsy will charge a 3.5% fee on the sale price. Now, if you want to at least make $500 per month then you will have to offer products that you think will be sold easily and give you the opportunity to make the earnings you require. The price stated on any item depends on the owner of the shop and if you think that your item is worth a big amount, you're free to post it as the sale price. This is an incredible opportunity for people to pursue their passion and enjoy their lives while doing so.

Way 4: Developing Career on oDesk – Selling Your Skills

oDesk is a short form of "online desk" referring to a place where an individual can work without the traditional obstructions. It is a highly professional network that deals with the buying and selling of diversified skills. You can utilize the skills that you have attained through all the learning and experience you have amassed in your life and earn an income without having to go to a specialized office and work within stern timings. It is today known as a global job marketplace where you can set up your desk and provide your skills to one who is in a need of them. If you have the skills, then you can easily find customers within the website who will be willing to pay you at your terms and conditions and even the work timings will be your decision.

Whether your skills pertains to web development, SEO articles, design and multimedia, business services, sales and marketing, or any other knowledgeable expertise that you might attain, oDesk is equipped with all the resources that one might need in order to convey the skills to others. Smartly utilizing your skills to earn a healthy amount is important and to achieve this you should pre-plan what your unique selling proposition will be. oDesk is especially popular for teamwork in which one individual hires a number of players to join one team to accomplish a given project. This way, diversification of team members is possible, and there arises no need of adjoining all of them together in one physical place, which would bear a high cost.

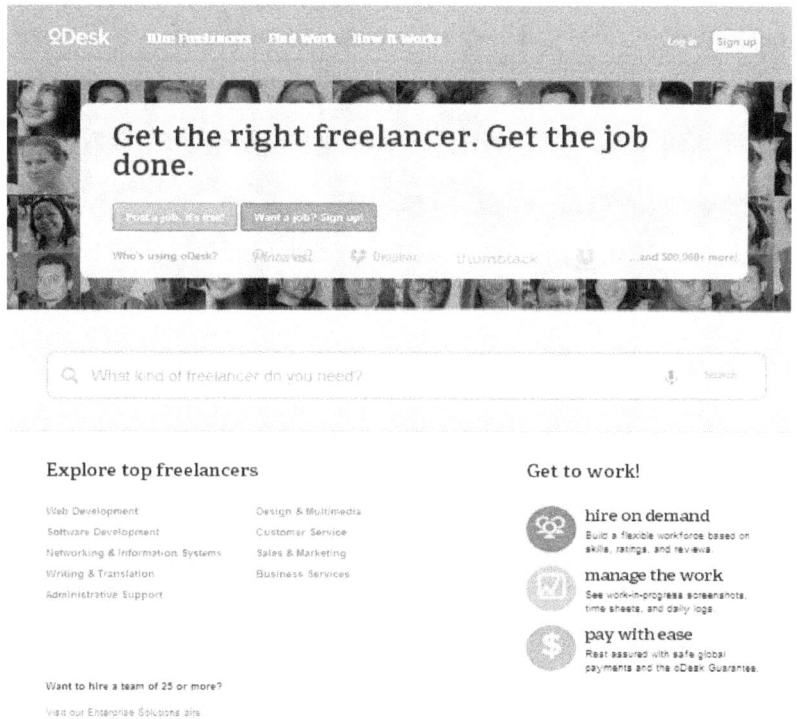

https://www.oDesk.com/

To get started you'll make your own profile and include all the highlights of your education and the skills that you have acquired. Your profile will attract customers to hire you when you bid on their project, so be very scrupulous when creating your profile, and perform the task very cleverly. To earn at least $500 you have to work on several projects, and you can receive that many tasks by bidding more on multiple projects, which you think you can successfully accomplish with good quality deliverance. Once you make a good impression and your client is satisfied, then the same client will probably hire you multiple times, so giving 100% at all times is essential.

In order to enhance your credibility, you can take the oDesk skills test, and results will be viewed by clients when they read through your profile. This will ensure clients that you have the potential to perform the work that you have opted for. In addition, posting a portfolio will help increase the value of your profile. It will include all of your previous work and projects that you have accomplished and even adding the link or images would be a good way to get your clients to trust your expertise.

Way 5: Are you A Creative Writer? Join iwriter.com or iNeedArticles

True professionalism is displayed on the writing website iwriter.com. Top freelancers use this site to perform tasks, which pay well. If you're particularly looking for a place where you can fully consume your writing skills then iwriter.com is the website you should be working with. It does not rely on bidding on projects; instead, the way projects are offered to an individual is dependent on their skills in writing. The better you write, the higher you are paid.

There are proper rating systems that iWriter.com equips itself with, and according to which you'll be able to choose the articles you want to write from the job desk. This is another advantage, as you will choose what you want to write unlike other websites in which tasks are given and you have to complete them whether you're interested in the topic or not. The tasks are displayed on the website, and one can view the complete instructions provided by the client and then decide to work on it. The ratings allow you to gradually decrease the workload, but still get paid more for writing better articles. The prime aim is to go that extra mile and deliver a good content article to your customer thus giving them a reason to come back to you.

http://www.iwriter.com/

https://ineedarticles.com/

INeedArticles.com is another site that you can also go to and write articles for money.

Each task that one writes will get rated and as the ratings of your profile increase, the higher paid jobs will be made accessible to you. Ineedarticles.com cuts 19% of the paid fee for the transaction charges, and the rest is your earned profit which can easily by multiplied by writing more and more articles in order to get a full $500 every month. If you're able to contend one particular customer, then he/she might even put a special request to only assign jobs to you, which by the way, offers a higher payment than the regular articles.

People enjoy earning appreciation for the incredible work that they do and believe that they are much better at something than others usually are. Ineedarticles.com takes special care of their prolific writes and thus the website displays the names of the most astounding writers on the main page. The ratings and their names are displayed right next to each other enabling clients to see the best of the best. The biggest advantage this gets in increasing the amount you earn is that clients will probably choose from these writers to get their content written. If you are one of the chosen, then you will definitely be receiving a higher amount for a higher number of articles written as a result of special requests.

Way 6: Fiverr.com Can Help a Lot

Earning an amount that one is aiming for is no more challenging than a job that requires lifting bricks, in a non-literal sense. Fiverr.com is a website, which provides an opportunity for two kinds of masses: the buyer and the seller. The focus here is primarily on how to get the seller to the podium where one can earn at least an amount of $500 per month. Fiverr.com offers diversified services for a total payment of $5. The services vary from professional work to moderate skills work. Many different services may be offered by a seller; regardless of the amount of skills or knowledge required to perform the job. The key is providing good quality services and ultimately keeping the customers happy and satisfied with the work.

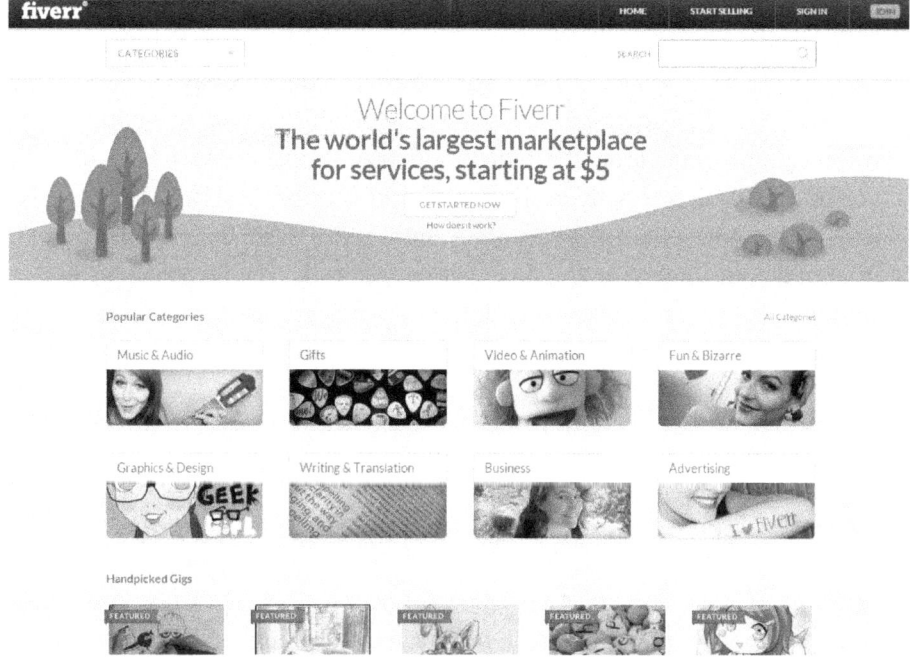

http://fiverr.com/

The biggest turnaround which fiverr.com provided on the stage was that it altered the entire procedure of buying and selling. Usually in websites like these, a prospect posts his/her work on which the buyer bids an amount and if the prospect is satisfied, then he accepts the bid and submits the work for completion to the buyer. However, in fiverr.com the buyer is put on the spot first giving a slight advantage to them. The buyer decides the kind of work that he or she is willing to perform, and the buyer then selects from the number of options available at the site. The higher the number of services one posts on the website, the higher the probability of getting chosen for tasks completion.

Suppose a person is working on one task for $5, eliminating $1 as a service tax, which fiverr.com cuts, leaving an actual $4 earned per task. Fiverr.com cuts about 20% for providing this incredible platform through which a person can earn up to as much as their potential allows. Coming to the point, $4 for one task means even if someone completes five $5 tasks a day that will generate earnings of $20 per day. Now, in order to accomplish the goal of at least making $500 per month a person only has to work 25 days. To increase the intervals of incoming payments, one can hire additional employees and complete more services on a daily basis.

To generate income successfully, a few tactical strategies have to be implemented. The first is to survey the market at fiverr.com by visiting their website and looking around for the products or services, which have the greatest demand. Secondly, analyzing the skills of one's self is also a crucial part, since underselling or overselling can create a destructive impression in front of the customers leading to negative feedback. The feedback on any work that is being bought or sold at fiverr.com is accessible to all the viewers and cannot be deleted by anyone except authorized workforces of fiverr.com.

One more option although not as popular is http://tenerr.com/

Way 7: Writing Kindle Books to Sell on Amazon

Writing kindle books can be very easy for people who are skilled in writing. Although the process of writing a book can be a lengthy one, Amazon has made publishing extremely simple. All the masses of people who are willing to self-publish their books and sell them to respective people, can post their kindle books on Amazon and get them sold at their own stated price.

Browse

Kindle Book Deals
  Kindle Daily Deals
  100 Books for $3.99 or Less
Popular Features
  Kindle Best Sellers
  Kindle Select 25
  New York Times® Best
  Sellers
  Editors' Picks
  Kindle Serials
  Kindle Singles
  Advanced Search
Categories
  Arts & Photography
  Biographies & Memoirs
  Business & Investing
  Children's Books
  Comics & Graphic Novels
  Computers & Technology
  Cookbooks, Food & Wine
  Crafts, Hobbies & Home
  eBooks Kindle en Español

Kindle eBooks

Kindle Daily Deals | 100 Books for $3.99 or Less | Best Sellers | Kindle Select 25 | Editors' Picks | Kindle S

More Items to Consider

You viewed   Customers who viewed this also viewed

Horses - For Kids -
Amazing Animal...
John Davidson, Annalee
Davidson, ...
★★★★★ (2)
Kindle Price: $2.99

Frogs - For Kids -
Amazing Animal...
John Davidson, Amazing
Animal Books
Kindle Price: $2.99

Spiders - For Kids -
Amazing Animal...
John Davidson, Amazing
Animal Books
Kindle Price: $2.99

Pandas - For Kids -
Amazing Animal...
John Davidson, Amazing
Animal Books
★★★★☆ (1)
Kindle Price: $2.99

› View or edit your browsing history

Kindle Select 25: 25 Exciting Books This Week

http://www.amazon.com/

The book, however, has to meet some basic requirements. One of them is the content's design and format. Formatting the text of your book should be very particular and similar in all pages. In addition, the images that you post of the book will only be displayed in grayscale so ensure that the pictures you chose do not rely much on color for an explanation. Grammar, spelling, and punctuation matter in any kind of writing and kindle books come under this scrutiny as well. Save the file on filtered HTML format because kindle books are to be viewed in that form only. Once that is done, you need to convert the document into an eBook in order to sell it through Amazon.

After the eBook is ready, you can publish it by stating your price and royalty information. Amazon takes under 48 hours to set the eBook on its sale list. You will get 70% of the stated price, so ensure that you make calculations first. The remaining 30% is kept by Amazon as a fee for providing the platform in which to sell in a much easier way. The number of books you sell will decide on how fast you'll be able to make $500 per month. There is no limit to the number of eBooks, you can put on sale, and this aspect makes it easier to make the desired amount of money. Of course, there has to be a lot of hard work and effort put in, but at the end of the day if the book sells, then all of that hard work has definitely paid off.

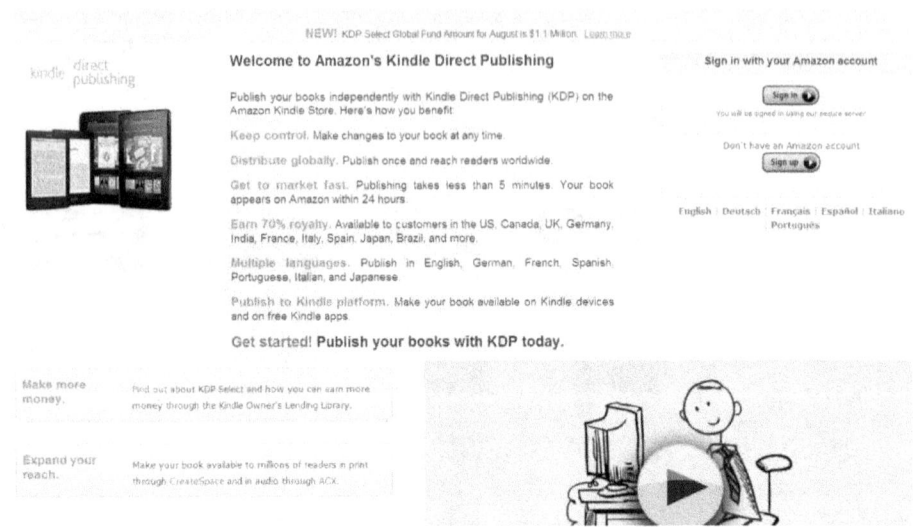

https://kdp.amazon.com/self-publishing/signin

The self-publishing of books has worked very well for me. I try to pace myself and write a couple of books a week. They are not huge books only around 8,000 to 10,000 words each and can be done in my spare time. If you are not a writer you can hire one to get this done and look at my other books on how to outsource this portion. Last year I produced over 100 books. The cost to produce and the rate of return on book publications is one of the best investments that I have found.

Here is my author link on Amazon.com so that you can see I write and publish books in a wide range of topics.

http://www.amazon.com/John-Davidson/e/B00BJPC1UC

Way 8: Have a Teaching Passion? Teach Others Online

With the entire amount of knowledge one can acquire from the internet you can easily use your understanding to your advantage. The best thing about having a familiarity with a certain topic is that you can convey it properly to others, so that they achieve the same understanding as yours. Many people know exactly how to make $500 per month and are earning that much from a variety of sources. As an example, a good opportunity for a person can involve making a digital piece on how to make $500 per month. Writing a short article will pass along general information, but if you have extensive knowledge then you can even write an eBook, which would mention many workable resources through which $500 can be earned every month. Moreover, videos can also be made explaining the procedures of each source meticulously. A monthly newsletter can be posted each month, describing a new way of earning $500 per month. You can have your own website and advertise it to generate traffic towards your website and generate $500 per month this way. You can become a consultant and help others set up their website or business to increase their income and they will pay you for this service.

Way 9: How You Can Flip Websites on Flippa

World Wide Web is known as a commonplace where buyers and sellers exchange their content in order to earn revenues and the content, which is not only useful for the buyer, is also profitable for the seller. Thousands of websites are being made and sold on daily a basis that are in competition with each other as they try to be on top of the charts. However, Flippa is the number 1 marketplace providing a platform in which to buy and sell websites. However, it is not only about what content is being sold or bought, but also about how the transactions are being done, which is where Flippa steps in and changes the game for all. The distinctive techniques that Flippa has brought forth to make money involve selling websites that boost the market for more opportunities. Some of these methods are:

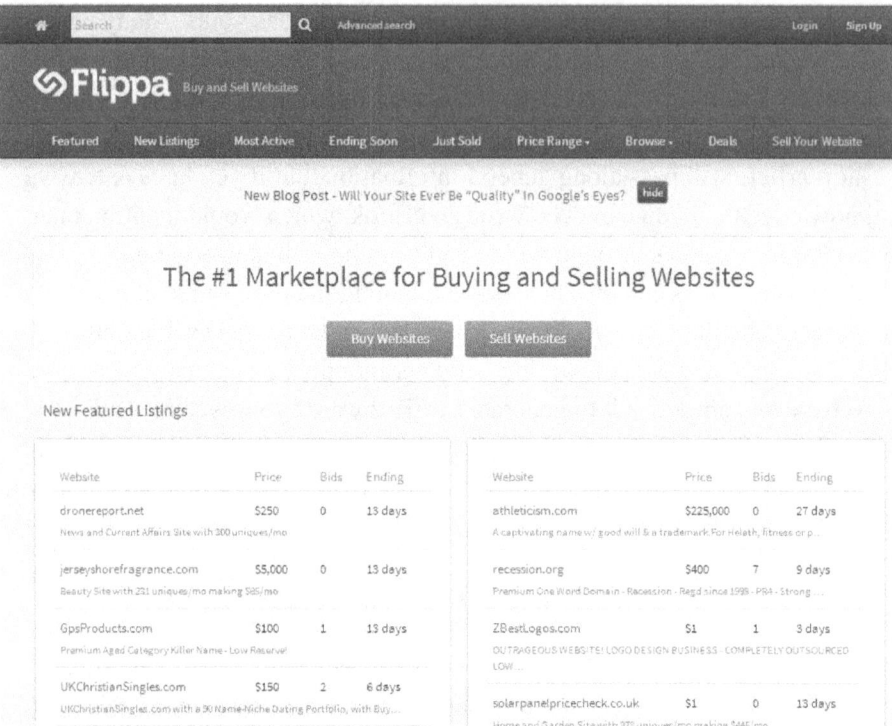

https://flippa.com/

1. Re-create the Old - One man's trash is another man's treasure –
    many websites listed on Flippa are ones that have been not in use
    for the longest time or are left by the wayside by owners who do not
    need them anymore. Website flippers then purchase these unused
    websites at the cheapest prices. They are then revamped to a
    completely new level, as the user requires and then sold to the
    respective customer for an additional price that calculates into
    profit. Here comes your opportunity to reshape a website that has
    already been built and since you don't have to start from scratch,
    basic knowledge of website creation is the prime skill required.
    Some of these websites lack either content or design, which is why
    they did not receive much traffic. Sometimes the owners start their
    website with a new concept and idea, but then run out of
    innovations causing it to fail to receive substantial traffic since users
    are always looking for new things. Your creativity and innovation

can help these clients maintain their websites in return for which you can generate an income.

All of this has an overall impact on the flippers, giving them a chance to utilize their skills and earn a healthy amount of money. Renovating these websites and marketing them in a fresh way would enable the website to strike more users and generate heavy traffic.

2. Another method that Flippa provides is starting a new website from scratch. This consumes more time and energy, but it also generates a lot more profit than the rehabilitation and sales of existing websites. In order to make your website more popular amongst the masses, first research the new trends that are capturing the market and include those in your website. In order to capture larger traffic for example, incorporate advertisements that have the highest click through rates or the comment boxes that determines people's feedback or online blogging that connects visitors to your website.

By using a combination of these methods, you can easily earn $500 per month. You can also acquire your own special clients who trust that you're a potential flipper, and thus only give their work to you.

Way 10: How to Double Your Money Using Online Resources

The above-mentioned are diversified sources with the help of which you can earn $500 from every other skill that you acquire. Any individual is not restricted to use any one website and there is no such thing as loyalty when it comes to earning money online. The smartest thing is to use a variety of websites and work with them altogether. This way there is an increased possibility of earning much more than $500 per month. If you're able to earn $500 by writing articles at iwriter and selling your arts and crafts or vintage items at an Etsy shop for another $500, then the cash you make eventually adds up. In this way, you can utilize each and every skill in full capacity to generate the income that you wish to have. The greatest advantage of online work is that of the time frame, which doesn't follow traditional 9-5 constraints of a job. You can work whenever, wherever and however you wish in order to get your job done when working online.

However, time management and delivery on time is very essential for customer satisfaction. Only take on jobs that you think you can accomplish at a given time. Sometimes even the smallest of jobs can take a lot of time so a good recommendation would be to not take on too many projects all at once. It is always a good idea to get familiarized with every job, one at a time, and then gradually increase your workload.

Chapter 7 - Reasons for Online Business Failure

As per statistics, 99.9% people fail to earn money through the internet and the reason is simple. Most people simply lack the initiative to get started. Even after conducting all of the research about this method of earning easy money, 99% of people won't even try to do it. ClickBank has a user base of more than 100,000 users, and almost all of them, who select a product or service and try to sell it, make some money. However, those who don't earn anything are the ones who don't start at all. Experiences have proven this phenomenon. You may have several friends and family members in your circle that may have tried to do online work, but simply did not initiate the process. Starting an online business is easy and quick. For instance, if you are interested in starting a web portal, it takes only two hours to set up your own web portal. This would include purchasing the domain name, finding a host, adding website content and activating the website for internet users.

It may take some time, because you should research and do your homework, before actually starting online work. The best way to learn and grow in this field is through trial and error and learning as you work. Practical knowledge is far more fruitful in this line of work than bookish education. You must decide now. Do you want to be a part of the ninety-nine percent, who lack the initiative to take action or do you want to join the 1% who are making huge amounts of money using this medium of business. Follow the guidelines described in this book and soon, you will be among the successful 1%.

Conclusion

This book has been an introduction to each of these different areas. If you would like more detailed instructions or help, please look at some of our other books on Amazon. We execute everything that we have talked about in this book to create income for our family and you can too. Pick one and learn how to make money with it and then move to the next one.

After reading all of these things, I hope you make up your mind now. Building a true extra income could be very lucrative because sometimes the money that you get could not be treated as **"extra"** anymore. If you are serious and professional in dealing some of your extra works, sooner or later your sweats from your hard work will be greatly paid, more than the money from your regular job.

After that, for sure the reasons that lead you to make some extra money will really be covered more than enough. At first you only wanted to pay your bills, save some money, make a project, or whatever purpose, but in the long run, your reasons can change.

The truth is that once you get serious about earning extra income, your view about finding money will change. From the time you will earn a lot through extra income only, and you can prove to yourself that you can live even without your full time job. Actually, there are many people who chose to monetize their own passion that started it as a side income or extra income. But, because they found out that they were more effective in doing that work, and that because it greatly pays too; then they stop from their regular jobs.

Well, this is not telling you or programming you to do the same, but this is a bright idea that brings some hope to you while building extra income. It is just like exploring your potentials that could be converted into cash. And later on you can use your skills and knowledge while you are making your extra cash for more income that you truly deserve.

Yes, you can do it because you have something within yourself. And that is about your longing to escape from money problems. That attitude makes you different from others because you are creative, resourceful, and a problem solver. So, keep on learning and keep on doing what you have learned. Just repeat what works for you and try finding new ways to improve what you have. Money will just come in freely the moment that you mastered your system in building extra income. Therefore, master your craft by executing what you learn and keep on trying different ways to find out what will best work for you. So, good luck and stay motivated!

Here is our Amazon Author page:

http://www.amazon.com/John-Davidson/e/B00BJPC1UC/ref=sr_tc_2_0?qid=1375372762&sr=8-2-ent

Here is one of our Clickbank sites:

http://www.housecabin.com/

We hope you gained ideas to help you generate income online and learned some valuable information from our book.

We have a blog that we update frequently that includes new ideas for making money online:

http://training.sdsplans.com/

Have a great day and enjoy making money online!

Author Bio

Saad Ghafoor

Education
Bachelors, Human Resource Management University of the Punjab
2010 - Present
High School, Computer Sciences Forman Christian College
2008 - 2010

Check out some of the other Entrepreneur Series books
Entrepreneur Series books on Amazon

Check out some of the Health Learning Series books
Health Learning Series on Amazon

Amazing Animal Books Series

How to Build and Plan Books

This book is published by

JD-Biz Corp

P O Box 374

Mendon, Utah 84325

http://www.jd-biz.com/

Read more books from John Davidson